For You

Balboa Press books may be ordered through booksellers or by contacting:

Balboa Press
A Division of Hay House
1663 Liberty Drive
Bloomington, IN 47403
www.balboapress.com
1 (877) 407-4847

ISBN: 978-1-4525-1836-7 (sc)
ISBN: 978-1-4525-1837-4 (e)

Printed in the United States of America.

Balboa Press rev. date: 11/5/2014

BALBOA
PRESS
A DIVISION OF HAY HOUSE

This is a book made with love and dedicated to all of you. I hope this book can serve as an inspirational reminder of all you can be.

May you live a most joyous life.

Note to the reader

The initial idea of this book, *For You,* was
to instil positive thinking in children by
reading them an inspirational quote every day,
accompanied by a beautiful illustration. While
children may not wholly understand the quote,
it is my hope that parents will be inspired to
explain the meaning through a story, guided by
the illustrations. What greater gift can a child
be given than the confidence and ability to
think positively throughout their lives.

Death is a stripping away of all that is not you. The secret of life is to "die before you die" – and find that there is no death.

The Power of Now
Echkart Tolle

For life and death are one, even as the river and the sea are one.

The Prophet
Kahlil Gibran

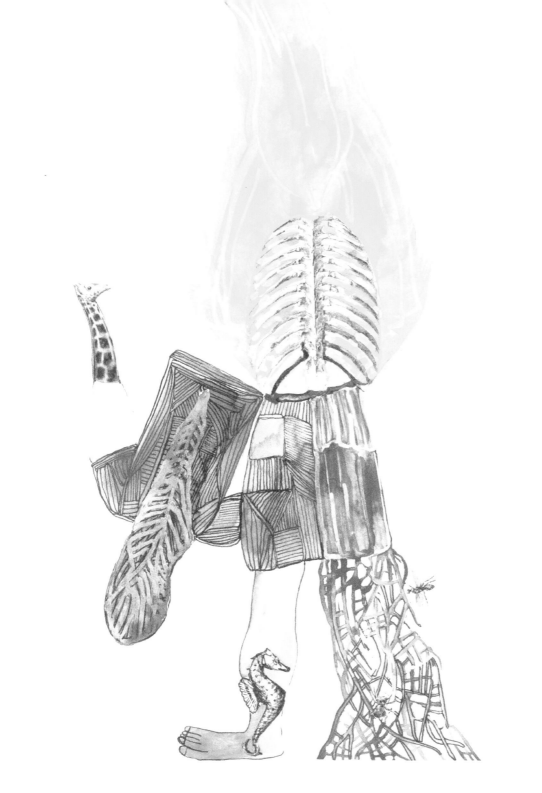

Learn to know thyself.

The Quran
Prophet Mohammed (P.B.U.H.)

*We need to forget what we think we are,
so that we can really become what we are.*

The Zahir
Paulo Coelho

Devotion is of the heart

*for at times, it is solely via the power
of the heart & Divine love that an
obstacle can be transcended.*

*Along the Path to Enlightenment,
365 Daily Reflections from David R. Hawkins, M.D., Ph.D.*
Dr. David R. Hawkins

Gender equality is critical to the development and peace of every nation.

Kofi Anan

As you grow up, always tell the truth,
do no harm to others, and don't think you are
the most important being on earth.
Rich or poor, you then can look anyone in
the eye and say, "I'm probably no better than
you, but I'm certainly your equal."

Harper Lee

Okay, we are different it's true.
And I don't like all the things that you do.
But here's one thing to think through,
You're a lot like me and I'm a lot like you!

Robert Alan Silverstein

*Do unto others
as you would have them
do unto you.*

Jesus Christ

When one realizes that one is the
universe – complete and at one with
All That Is, forever without end –
no further suffering is possible.

Power vs. Force
Dr. David R. Hawkins

*You know you are
on the road to success if you would
do your job and not be paid for it.*

Oprah Winfrey

See God
in every person,
place and thing,
and all will be well
in your world.

Louise Hay

All major religious traditions carry basically the same message that is love, compassion & forgiveness. The important thing is they should be part of our daily lives.

His Holiness the 14th Dalai Lama

Do not dwell in the past,
do not dream of the future,
concentrate the mind on the present moment.

Gautama Siddharta Buddha
563 BC–483 BC

Give up defining yourself – to yourself or to others. You won't die. You will come to life. And don't be concerned with how others define you. When they define you, they are limiting themselves, so it's their problem. Whenever you interact with people, don't be there primarily as a function or a role but as the field of conscious presence. You can only lose something that you have but you cannot lose something that you are.

A New Earth: Awakening to Your Life's Purpose
Eckhart Tolle

To be one, to be united is a great thing. But to respect the right to be different is maybe even greater.

Bono

Love is not selective, just as the light
of the sun is not selective.
It does not make one person special.
It is not exclusive. Exclusivity is not the
love of God but the "love" of ego.
However, the intensity with which true love is
felt can vary. There may be one person
who reflects your love back to you more clearly
and more intensely than others, and if that
person feels the same towards you, it can be
said that you are in a love relationship with
him or her. The bond that connects you with
that person is the same bond that connects you
with the person sitting next to you on a bus, or
with a bird, a tree, a flower.
Only the degree of intensity with which
it is felt differs.

The Power of Now: A Guide to Spiritual Enlightenment
Eckhart Tolle

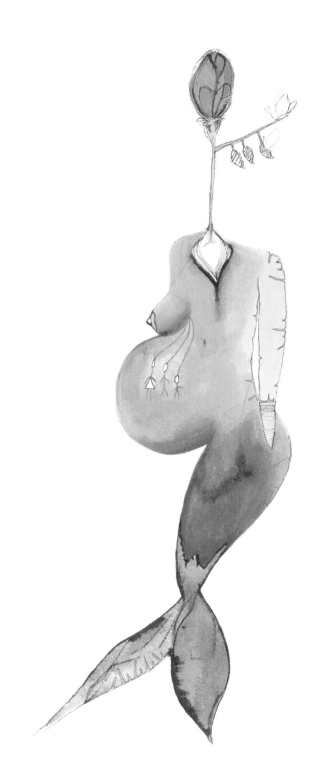

I am the hole in the flute that God's breath flows through

Eckhart Tolle

Heaven on Earth
is a choice you must make,
not a place you must find.

Dr. Wayne Dyer

The only way to get what you really want is to let go of what you don't want.

Iyanla Vanzant

Family is the most important thing in the world.

Princess Diana
1961–1997

One cannot help but be in awe when he contemplates the mysteries of eternity, of life, of the marvellous structure of reality. It is enough if one tries merely to comprehend a little of this mystery every day.

Albert Einstien
1879–1955

*Humankind has not woven
the web of life. We are but
one thread within it.
Whatever we do to the web,
we do to ourselves.
All things are bound together,
all things are connected.*

Chief Seattle
1780–1866

Ask and it will be given to you,
seek and you will find;
knock and the door will be opened to you.

Jesus Christ

The little child before you is your favourite
teddy bear, your inner child.
What could you give him but love?

Jaya Mehra

You are the power in your world!
You get to have whatever you choose to think.

Louise Hay

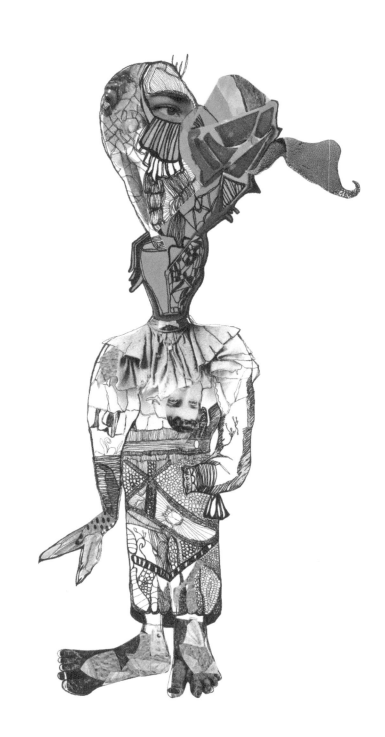

It is a man's own mind
not his enemy or foe,
that lures him to evil ways.

Gautama Siddharta Buddha
563 BC–483 BC

This above all:
To thine own self be true,
and it must follow,
as the night the day,
thou canst not be false to any man.

William Shakespeare

You are what you
believe yourself to be.

The Witch of Portobello
Paulo Coelho

Keep your thoughts positive because your
thoughts become your words.

Keep your words positive because your words
become your behaviours.

Keep your behaviours positive because your
behaviours become your habits.

Keep your habits positive because your
habits become your values.

Keep your values positive because your
values become your destiny.

Mahatma Gandhi

He who lives in harmony with himself lives in harmony with the universe.

Marcus Aurelius
121–180

Mind is the master power that moulds and makes and man is mind, and evermore he takes, the tool of thought, and, shaping what he wills, brings forth a thousand joys, a thousand ills. He thinks in secret, and it comes to pass, environment is but his looking glass.

James Allen
1864–1912

Choose a job you love, and you'll never have to work a day in your life.

Confucious

551 BC–479 BC

We are what we repeatedly do. Excellence then, is not an action, but a habit.

Aristotle
348 BC–322 BC

*The simple things are also
the most extraordinary things,
and only the wise can see them.*

The Alchemist
Paulo Coelho

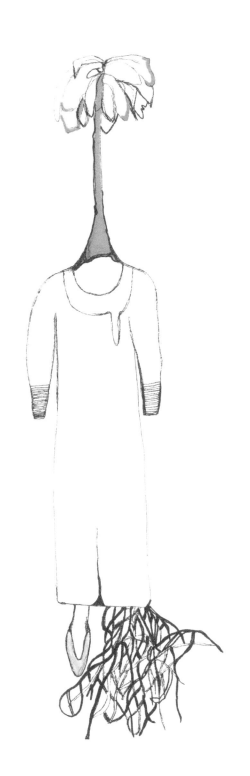

It is not the magnitude of our actions but the amount of love that is put into them.

Mother Teresa

*Every man's life
is a fairy tale written
by God's finger.*

Hans Christian Anderson
1805–1875

*Throw your soul
through every open door,
Count your blessings
to find what you look for.*

Rolling in the Deep
Adele Laurie Blue Adkin

Knock, and he'll open the door.
Vanish, and he'll make
you shine like the sun.
Fall, and he'll raise you to the heavens.
Become nothing, and he'll
turn you into Everything.

Jalal ad-Din Muhammad Rumi
1207–1273

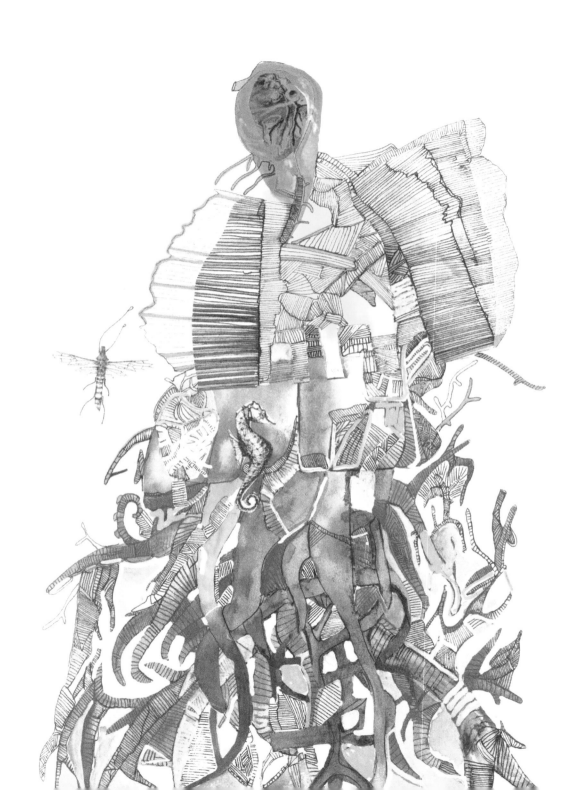

Faith is taking the
first step, even when
you don't see the whole staircase.

Martin Luther King Jr.
1929–1968

The minute I heard my first
love story, I started looking for you,
not knowing how blind that was.
Lovers don't finally meet somewhere.
They are in each other all along.

Jalal ad-Din Muhammad Rumi
1207–1273

We are what we think.
All that we are arises with our thoughts.
With our thoughts, we make the world.

Gautama Siddharta Buddha
563 BC–483 BC

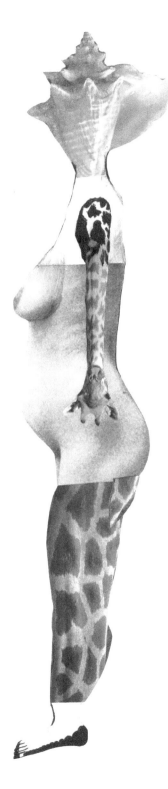

*If you can image it,
you can achieve it.
If you can dream it,
you can become it.*

William Arthur Ward
1921–1994

A ship is safe in harbour,
but that's not what ships are for.

William Shedd
1820–1894

Every breath we take,
every step we make,
can be filled with
peace, joy & serenity.
We need only to be awake,
alive in the present moment.

Peace is Every Step: The Path of Mindfulness in Everyday Life
Thich Nhat Hanh

The whole secret of
existence is to have no fear.
Never fear what will become
of you, depend on no one.
Only the moment you reject
all help are you freed.

Gautama Siddharta Buddha
563 BC–483 BC

You've done it before and you can do it now. See the positive possibilities. Redirect the substantial energy of your frustration and turn it into positive, effective, unstoppable determination.

Ralph Marston

All things are bound together,
all things connect.
Whatever befalls the earth,
befalls also the children of the earth.

Onandaga Nation
Chief Oren Lyons

We may have different religions,
different languages, different
coloured skin, but we all belong
to one human race.

Kofi Annan

Our task must be to free ourselves
by widening our circle of compassion
to embrace all living creatures and the
whole of nature and its beauty.

Albert Einstein
1879–1955

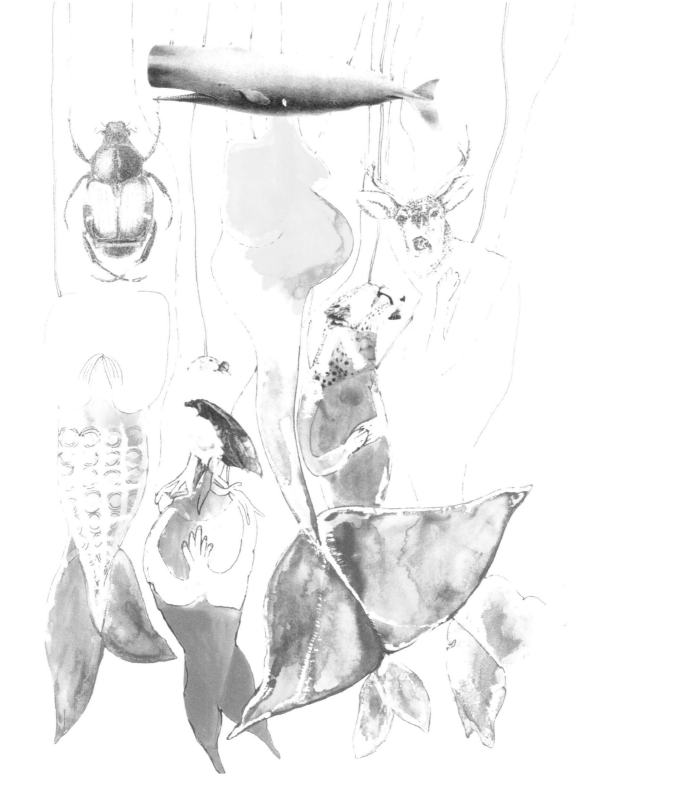

Flee from hate, mischief and jealousy. Don't bury your thoughts, put your vision to reality. Wake up and live.

Bob Marley
1945–1981

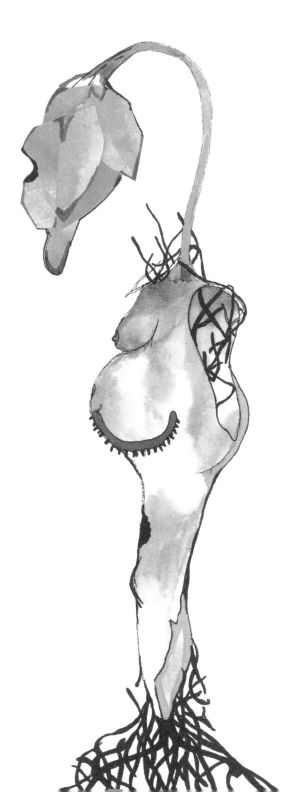

You've gotta dance like nobody's watching, love like you'll never be hurt, sing like there's nobody listening, and live like it's heaven on earth.

William W. Purkey

Count your blessings
& be grateful for everything

Thank You

*God for honouring me with inspiration
to serve Thee more with this book.
Thank you for bringing me all the
support and love through my friends
and family members. I express my
gratitude to you all.*

Amalie-Suhaila Beljafla

was born the 11th of May 1991 she comes from a
Scandinavian and Arabic background. After graduating
from Dubai International Academy with an I.B diploma,
Amalie moved to London to pursue her degree at
London's prestigious art university, Central Saint Martins
in 2009. Having completed a foundation degree in
Art and Design, she continued her BA in Graphic Design,
finishing with an honors degree in June 2013.
She is currently doing her MA in Communication
and Design, graduating in June 2015.

She has collaborated with various artists as
well as fashion designers, and in 2012 ventured out
to start her own fashion house, Trésors Sauvages,
www.tresorssauvages.com, and is beginning a new project
with one other entrepreneur, Leda And The Swan LTD,
www.ledaandtheswan.org, which will be a boutique in London.
In 2014 Amalie started her own swimwear and
resort brand called AMALIE, *www.amalieresort.co.uk*
to be launched Summer 2014.

Amalie supports the charity Signal,
www.signalethiopia.org, and some of the proceeds
of this book will go towards the charity.

For You is Amalie's first book.

www.amaliesbook.com
www.amalie-suhaila.com
www.tresorssauvages.com
www.amaliesresort.co.uk
www.krcbyamalie.com
www.ledaandtheswan.org
www.amaliebeljafla.com

CPSIA information can be obtained at www.ICGtesting.com
Printed in the USA
LVOW02s1922260415

436088LV00006B/11/P

9 781452 518367